About The Wiener Library

The Wiener Library is one of the world's leading and most extensive archives on the Holocaust and Nazi era. Formed in 1933, the Library's unique collection of over one million items includes published and unpublished works, press cuttings, photographs and eyewitness testimony.

Our vision is of a continuously developing library, archive and information service for the UK and for the international community, dedicated to supporting research, learning, teaching and advocacy about the Holocaust and genocide, their causes and consequences.

The Wiener Library
for the Study of the Holocaust & Genocide
29 Russell Square
London WC1B 5DP
www.wienerlibrary.co.uk

 facebook.com/wienerlibrary
 @wienerlibrary
 @wienerlibrary

About The Holocaust Research Institute at Royal Holloway, University of London

The Holocaust Research Institute at Royal Holloway, University of London, is the leading academic centre of its kind in Europe. Founded in 2000, we are internationally recognised for our research, teaching, public advocacy and creative work.

The Research Institute's mission is to promote research into the Holocaust, its origins and aftermath, and to examine the extent to which genocide, war and dictatorship can be understood as defining elements in the history of the twentieth century. It is an international, interdisciplinary forum, bringing together researchers working on different aspects of the Holocaust in areas including history, literary and language studies, film and media studies, philosophy and sociology.

The Holocaust Research Institute
Royal Holloway, University of London
Egham Surrey TW20 0EX
Tel: +44 (0)1784 443310

 facebook.com/rhulhri
 @RHUL_HRI
 @RHUL_HRI

Introduction

I always thought I knew about my family story. And then I read Philippe Sands' wonderful book *East West Street* and realised that I didn't.

I knew what had happened to my maternal grandfather, Alfred Wiener, and his daughters. I knew how his wife, weakened by starvation, had died in Switzerland, only just having seen her children to safety from Bergen-Belsen. And I knew, too, the fate of my mother's aunt, uncle and cousin after their transportation.

On my father's side I had grown up with the tale of his exile to the borders of Siberia with his mother, when Stalin imprisoned my paternal grandfather in a Soviet labour camp. And I learned their incredible story of reunion when, quite by chance, my grandfather's friend found news of his family in a letter which had been sent far and wide in desperation and, for want of anything better to do with it, was affixed to the post office door.

So, as I say, I thought I knew my family story. But when I read Philippe's book on the terrible Nazi murders in Lwów, I began to gain new appreciation.

I realised that I had a large family - of great aunts, great uncles and cousins who disappeared after the Germans took over in Lwów. Of this tragedy we hadn't spoken. These relatives, dozens of them, were missing. Almost all of them murdered I presume, but where? When?

And, in exchanges with the author, I realised that it is very likely that Philippe and I are probably related, quite possibly sharing the same great-great-grandparents. We had gone to the same school together and spoken often professionally without knowing we were cousins.

In other words, I know so much but there is so much still to know, so much still to find out, so much still to trace.

Even now.

My story, of course, is just one tiny, tiny piece of the vast story that this exhibition seeks to bring to public attention. The tale of the Holocaust didn't stop when it finished. There was so much still to happen.

That is the power of the story these exhibits tell. They help visitors understand the sheer confusion and the heartbreak and hope that accompanied it as families sought to find each other if there was anyone to find, or, in so many cases, just to find out what happened.

At home I have the telegram that this Library's founder received in New York, informing him that his children were safe and then adding, curtly and without ceremony or commiseration, that his wife had died and been buried.

For most there was not even this, only a terrible silence. The effort to fill this void, to trace, to inform and to reunite was therefore a great humanitarian effort. And also a gargantuan task. Many of the records that did exist were not completely accurate. The initial trace of my mother suggests she could be found in Palestine, a place she had never visited.

To untangle all of this has been the work of decades.

A final point. Among the many justifications and beneficial effects of the work of Alfred Wiener and his many colleagues and successors, the need to trace people stands high upon the list. It is wonderful that the records are now sited at the Wiener Library, where they belong.

Lord Daniel Finkelstein OBE is a British journalist and politician. He is the Associate Editor of *The Times*, where he is also a weekly political columnist and leader writer. He was adviser to both Prime Minister John Major and Conservative leader William Hague and was also a member of the Prime Minister's Holocaust Commission. He is the grandson of Dr. Alfred Wiener, founder of The Wiener Library.

By 1945, Europe was in chaos. Millions of people had been murdered or displaced by war and genocide. Many were missing, with the fates of some remaining undetermined more than seventy years later.

The Allies tried to cope with the war's aftermath, including masses of people on the move. For many Holocaust survivors, the possibility of finding loved ones was a primal need and took precedence over everything else.

Different charities and agencies, such as the British Red Cross Society, attempted to help find the missing. Their efforts came together as the International Tracing Service (ITS).

This exhibition examines the complicated history of the search for the missing after the Holocaust.

Missing since September 1943, Zuzana Knobloch (née Hartmann), a young Czech Jew, was arrested in Prague with her husband, Ferdinand, for resistance and rescue activities. Zuzana's parents were murdered after being deported from Theresienstadt in 1942. It took her surviving family many decades to uncover her fate.

© WL Photo Archive

A postwar Czech index revealed that Zuzana Knobloch had been deported to Auschwitz-Birkenau on 25 November 1943. It is presumed that she died there.
© WL ITS Digital Archive 4999265

Liberation?

At war's end, millions of people were somewhere other than where they wanted to be. For Jewish survivors, especially those from Eastern Europe, the future was uncertain. The search for family members and friends drove many survivors to return home, even in defiance of military efforts to control the movement of people. When some did reach home, they found their communities destroyed and family missing. They often faced hostility and violence.

Allied militaries confronted daunting challenges. They needed to aid Displaced Persons (DPs) and help relieve disease and hunger. They aimed to regulate the movement of people so that military operations could continue. Their initial aim was to repatriate as many people as possible.

For a time, these goals were prioritised over finding missing people and reuniting families, even though military forces received many requests to find the missing.

Several charities and organisations tried to help within post-war occupied Europe and beyond. With no central authority in place, relatives approached as many organisations as possible with information about the last known whereabouts of family members.

'It was a colossal task to discover the surname, Christian name, date and place of birth, last known address and next of kin of every single living person in the camp – it was absolutely impossible to get accurate information about the dead…I almost despaired at the seemingly endless difficulties; information written on dreadful old scraps of paper in a dozen languages…Thousands of people wanted to know whether we had found any trace of this or that missing relative or friend.'

Evelyn Bark CMG OBE, British Red Cross

Władysław Lukrec launched a search for his son, Tadeusz, on 9 February 1946, writing to as many organisations as he could. Tadeusz had been imprisoned in Auschwitz, Gross-Rosen, and Buchenwald and Władysław desperately sought his whereabouts. Documents in the International Tracing Service archive do not reveal whether father and son were reunited.

© WL ITS Digital Archive 90583911

WŁADYSŁAW LUKREC, Ing.

9-th. February 1946
1, Pieracki street
Sosnowiec /Poland/

The
War Criminal Investigation
of the 3-th Army, Wiesbaden

GENTLEMEN,

I take the liberty of troubling you with a matter which I have much at heart.

My only son, Tadeusz Lukrec, born 31-th October 1923 was prisoner till December 1944 at the concentration camp Oświęcim /German name Auschwitz/ his prisoner s number 119 541. Subsequently he was deported to the concentration camp Gross Rosen, Workcommand Lissa Breslau, prisoner s number 91 050, and then in January to the Buchenwald, block 65, prisoner s number 128 581. There he was till last few days before the conquest of that camp by the American Forces.

According to the informations I did collect my son is not in the evidence of prisoners who got their liberation in Buchenwald. Therefore I may suppose that he was deported the 9-th April to the camp Dachau.

I am convinced that your help would be most effected in search for my son. Above all I beg you to inform me whether my son got his liberation in Dachau.

I end in the sincere hope that you will not refuse your assistance in this matter.

I trust the importance of the matter will be my best excuse for troubling you with it, and awaiting your kind reply, I remain

My Gentlemen,
Yours faithfully

P.S. I beg you to send the answer on double ways:
1./ direct to my pointed adress and
2./ by the Section of the Polish Red Cross in Vienna III, Rennweg

Images of the cruelty the Allies confronted at the liberation, like this of two surviving inmates of Nordhausen, are well known. Less well known are the efforts made by survivors and different organisations to search for the missing after the war. Nordhausen, 14 April 1945.
© WL Photo Archive

Silesian refugees look for relatives on lists of survivors.
Silesia, c. 1945
© USHMM, courtesy of Joseph Eaton

HIAS (Hicem)

Vertretungen
in allen Teilen der Welt

SUCHE NACH VERWANDTEN

in allen Laendern der Erde

Individuelle Hilfsgesuche

an Angehoerige

SAMMELTELEGRAMME   AUSKUENFTE

wegen Weiterwanderung

Zuverlaessige Informationen ueber
Einreisebestimmungen sowie Lebensbedingungen
in ueberseeischen Laendern

Zentrale Shanghai:
24 Central Road, Room 206

Zweigstelle Hongkew:
599 Tongshan Road, House 92

The search for family members was global. This Hebrew Immigrant Aid Society (HIAS) advertisement was published in a German Jewish refugee newspaper in Shanghai. The German text reads, 'HIAS (HICEM) representatives in all parts of the world search for relatives in all countries of the world. Individual help in searching for relatives. Collective telegrams, information about further emigration. Reliable information about immigration requirements as well as living conditions in overseas countries.'
c. 1945–48
© USHMM, courtesy Ralph Harpuder

This advertisement was placed by Sara and Irena Ceder in Tel Aviv in a Yiddish newspaper in New York. They were searching for their aunt and uncle, Franya and Filip Klein. c. 1950
© USHMM

Even before the liberation of Bergen-Belsen, inmates compiled lists of survivors. After the liberation, these lists formed the basis of tracing work in the Displaced Persons camp set up there. The United Nations Relief and Rehabilitation Administration (UNRRA), the British Red Cross, the Jewish Relief Unit, and the American Joint Distribution Committee helped administer the camp. The retreating Germans had destroyed most of the camp's records.
© WL Photo Archive

German Jewish refugee Senta Hirtz returned to Germany to work for one of the first Jewish Relief Unit teams sent to Bergen-Belsen in 1945. She described survivors' needs: 'There was one outstanding wish apart from the clothing; Do help us to find our relatives…I heard from my brother or uncle or so-and-so who lives at Camp Munich…help me to go there.'

Senta Hirtz
© WL Photo Archive

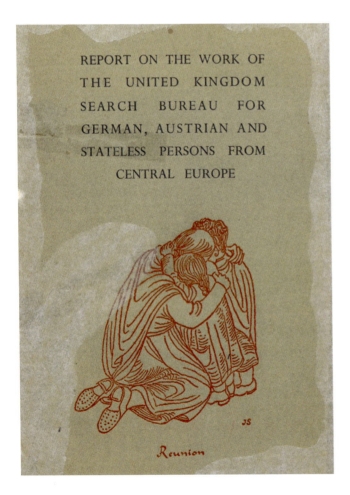

As early as 1943, a number of organisations in the UK met to discuss the creation of a centralised Search Bureau. Chaired by Otto Schiff, who supported Jewish refugees who came to Britain, the organisations included the Quakers, the British Cross Society, Association of Jewish Refugees and the Women's Voluntary Services. This report for June 1944 – April 1946 was prepared to document the efforts of the UK Search Bureau during this period.
© WL Collections

WAR ORGANISATION
OF THE
BRITISH RED CROSS SOCIETY and ORDER OF ST. JOHN OF JERUSALEM

FOREIGN RELATIONS DEPARTMENT

Chairman:
MAJ.-GENERAL SIR JOHN KENNEDY, K.B.E., C.B., C.M.G., D.S.O.
Director:
MISS S. J. WARNER, O.B.E.

Allied Prisoners of War Packing Centre
Heads of Packing Centre:
MRS. GRAZEBROOK
MRS. SECKER

TELEPHONE NO.:
Regent 0211   ABBEY 2511/5
Wimborne ~~CLARENCE~~ HOUSE.
Arlington Street, ~~ST. JAMES'S~~. LONDON, S.W.1

PLEASE QUOTE REF.
ESS/ONA

17624

23rd August, 1945

Dr. K. Fraustaedter
39, Aberdare Gardens
N.W.6

Dear Sir,

We have received two postcards from Berta Fraustaedter, recently liberated from the German concentration camp at Theresienstadt one directed to "Dr. med. Kurt Fraustaedter, London", the other to ourselves asking for news of him and of Hans Fraustaedter and Lotte Oppenheim.

We think that this probably refers to you, and if you will be good enough to confirm this and your present address, the cards will be forwarded to you immediately.

Yours faithfully

E. S. Scroggs
p.p. (M.R. Carden)

German and Austrian Jewish refugees who had come to England before the war wrote to a variety of agencies to learn about the fates of relatives who remained on the Continent. Berta Fraustaedter's children, Lotte, Kurt and Hans, had fled Nazi Germany. With the assistance of the British Red Cross Society and the Friends' Ambulance Unit, among others, they learned that their mother, Berta, had survived Theresienstadt. Her name appeared on a list of Berliners published by the World Jewish Congress in the *Aufbau*, a journal for German-speaking Jews founded in 1934.
© WL Collections

Organising chaos

International cooperation among charities and other bodies was key to facilitating tracing efforts. Some Displaced Persons arranged their own search organisations and compiled lists of survivors. Relief organisations, such as the Jewish Relief Unit, tried to help. Authorities recognised the need to centralise search efforts, which often duplicated activities or worked at cross purposes.

After the war, military authorities aimed to control searching to regulate the movement of refugees. They also wanted to track and limit information that was being shared across borders. The Cold War was developing. The Soviet Union withdrew its cooperation when it realised Soviet citizens were permitted to resettle in Western countries on political grounds.

The Central Tracing Bureau (CTB) coordinated initiatives among national and zonal tracing offices by July 1945. The CTB was the predecessor to what came to be known as the International Tracing Service. Lists compiled by various charities and organisations were gathered by the CTB and used in its tracing work.

The Search Bureau for Missing Relatives was created in 1945 by the Jewish Agency for Palestine to help relatives find each other. It published lists of names in a weekly bulletin called "To the Near and Far" and broadcast names over the radio.
1957 © Central Zionist Archives

CORC/P(45) 54

DIRECTORATE OF PRISONERS OF WAR AND DISPLACED PERSONS

Recommendations of the Directorate regarding the Establishment of a Central Tracing Service for United Nations' Missing in Occupied Germany

NOTE: This paper has been coordinated with the Political, Military, and Internal Affairs and Communications Divisions of the four National Elements of the Allied Control Authority and they concur therein.

Objectives

1. Recommended that the following should be the objectives of the Tracing Service:

   (a) to search for and trace military and civilian missing of the United Nations;
   (b) to establish, where possible, the fate of those missing who cannot be found alive;
   (c) to locate, collect and preserve all available records regarding displaced persons in Germany;
   (d) to serve as a link to bring interested persons into communication with each other.

National Tracing Bureau

2. Recommended that each interested United Nation that has not already established a National Tracing Bureau within its own national boundaries should be invited to establish such a Bureau, which should receive all initial enquiries concerning missing of its own nationality.

Zonal Search Bureaux

3. Recommended:

   (a) that these Bureaux (which are already established in each Zone) should assume responsibility for instituting searches in their own Zones, including searches on all enquiries passed to them by the Central Tracing Bureau;

   (b) that each Zonal Bureau should operate under the complete jurisdiction of its own Zone Commander subject only to the general policies of the Allied Control Council and the Central Tracing Policy Board. (See below.)

Central Tracing Bureau

4. Recommended:

   (a) that the Allied Control Council should be requested to invite UNRRA to place the Central Tracing Bureau and Associated Central Records Office, which it is already operating, at the Council's disposal to be operated by UNRRA under policies and directives issued by the Central Tracing Policy Board;

   (b) that the Central Bureau should operate as a central clearing house between the Zonal and National Bureaux and not as an executive body; it should not, therefore, issue policies and directives to the Zonal Bureaux, this being the task of the Central Tracing Policy Board.

Initially, the Allies envisaged a situation whereby each Allied nation would establish its own National Tracing Bureau (NTB) and the Central Tracing Bureau would act as a central 'clearing house' for cases which they could not solve or which required the cooperation of several NTBs.

Col. Bowring, head of the CTB, with a chart showing how NTBs work, 1948.
© United Nations Archives

The International Committee of the Red Cross (ICRC) seemed to be the natural agency to take responsibility for tracing after the war. However, its 'neutral humanitarianism' was at odds with the Allies' insistence that the Central Tracing Bureau would not deal with German POWs or civilians – this would be the task of the German Red Cross. The Allies also prioritised repatriating Displaced Persons, which was officially outside of the ICRC's remit.
© Courtesy, British Red Cross Museum and Archives

In January 1946, centralised tracing was moved from near Frankfurt to Arolsen, Germany, which was more or less undamaged at the end of the war. Thirty miles west of Kassel, it was close to the borders of the US, British and Soviet occupation zones. It had been a Nazi stronghold during the war, and initially, a former SS barracks was used to store documentation used for tracing.
© International Tracing Service, Bad Arolsen

Administration of the International Tracing Service

The Central Tracing Bureau (in 1948, renamed the International Tracing Service) had been administered by different institutions since the end of the war. In 2012, the ICRC resigned from managing the ITS, because the ITS had expanded from processing tracing requests to include opening its archives for research, education and commemoration. The German Federal archives is the institutional partner of the ITS. The ITS is overseen by an International Commission, including representatives of the United Kingdom.

1944–45
Supreme Headquarters Allied Expeditionary Forces

1945–47
United Nations Relief and Rehabilitation Administration

1947–51
International Refugee Organization

1951–55
Allied High Commission for Germany

1955–2012
International Committee of the Red Cross

Anna Charlotte Oppenheimer (née Fels) lived in Berlin and had one son, Rolf Guenther. Although her son managed to emigrate to England in August 1939, Anna remained behind. In April 1942, Rolf sent a telegram to his mother via the Red Cross. It stated: 'It has been a while since I've heard from you. Hope all is well.'

© WL Photo archives

Anna Charlotte Oppenheimer was deported from Berlin on 12 March 1943 on Transport 36 to Auschwitz-Birkenau, where she likely was murdered.
© WL ITS Digital Archive, 11193892

HELP WANTED

In an effort to bring together again thousands of lonely unhappy people who are to-day searching for one another across the International frontiers of Europe and Asia, an earnest appeal is being made to all members of the general public to give every help possible so that separated families and parted friends may once more be reunited.

During six long years of total war vast numbers of ordinary law-abiding citizens were uprooted from their homes, and parted from their dear ones. Many men, women and young children were taken out of their own countries to perform slave labour in foreign lands. Tiny babies were forced from their mothers' arms and brought into Hitler's Germany to become citizens of the Third Reich. Hundreds of thousands of foreigners died in concentration camps; on death marches; in over crowded transports; in hospitals; in prisons; in factories and labour gangs.

To-day the survivors of this, the worlds greatest population transfer, are desperately seeking the lost members of their scattered families. Many of those sought are probably now dead, but their deaths have not been legally confirmed so that wills cannot be proved or fresh marriages contracted by widows and widowers.

It is to assist the gigantic task of establishing the fate of all those persons whose names are now listed amongst the legion of the lost, that UNRRA Central Tracing Bureau is asking for the help of every generous hearted person who is in a position to assist.

1.   Continued............

Continued:

Such help can be given by private persons who have in their possession:-

1). Any information concerning children who were forcibly separated from their parents, and removed out of their own countries.

2). Any knowledge of the names and circumstances of death of prisoners who died in concentration camps, on death marches; in over-crowded transports; or during work in factories and labour gangs.

3). Any documents, identity papers of foreigners; camp, hospital, crematoria and prison records; clothing and personal effects of foreigners who were in Germany between the years 1938 - 1945.

4). Any knowledge of unmarked single or mass graves which may contain the body of a foreigner, or of a political or Jewish persecutee.

Members of the general public may all unwittingly be keeping as curiosities and souvenirs some such items as those mentioned, without realising how valuable such things may prove to be in establishing the fate or whereabouts of a lost person. One document, one piece of clothing, one pocket book or letter, may be the clue or missing link which will bring joy, peace and happiness to minds now tortured by worry, uncertainty and anxiety.

Therefore, it is most strongly urged that every type of information and every sort of objective evidence be submitted immediately for examination by UNRRA Central Tracing Bureau Arolsen by Kassel, Germany.

2.

The Central Tracing Bureau issued this appeal after the war. "It is to assist the gigantic task of establishing the fate of all those persons whose names are now listed among the legion of the lost, that UNRRA Central Tracing Bureau is asking for the help of every generous hearted person who is in a position to assist."
© WL ITS Digital Archive, 82501231-32.

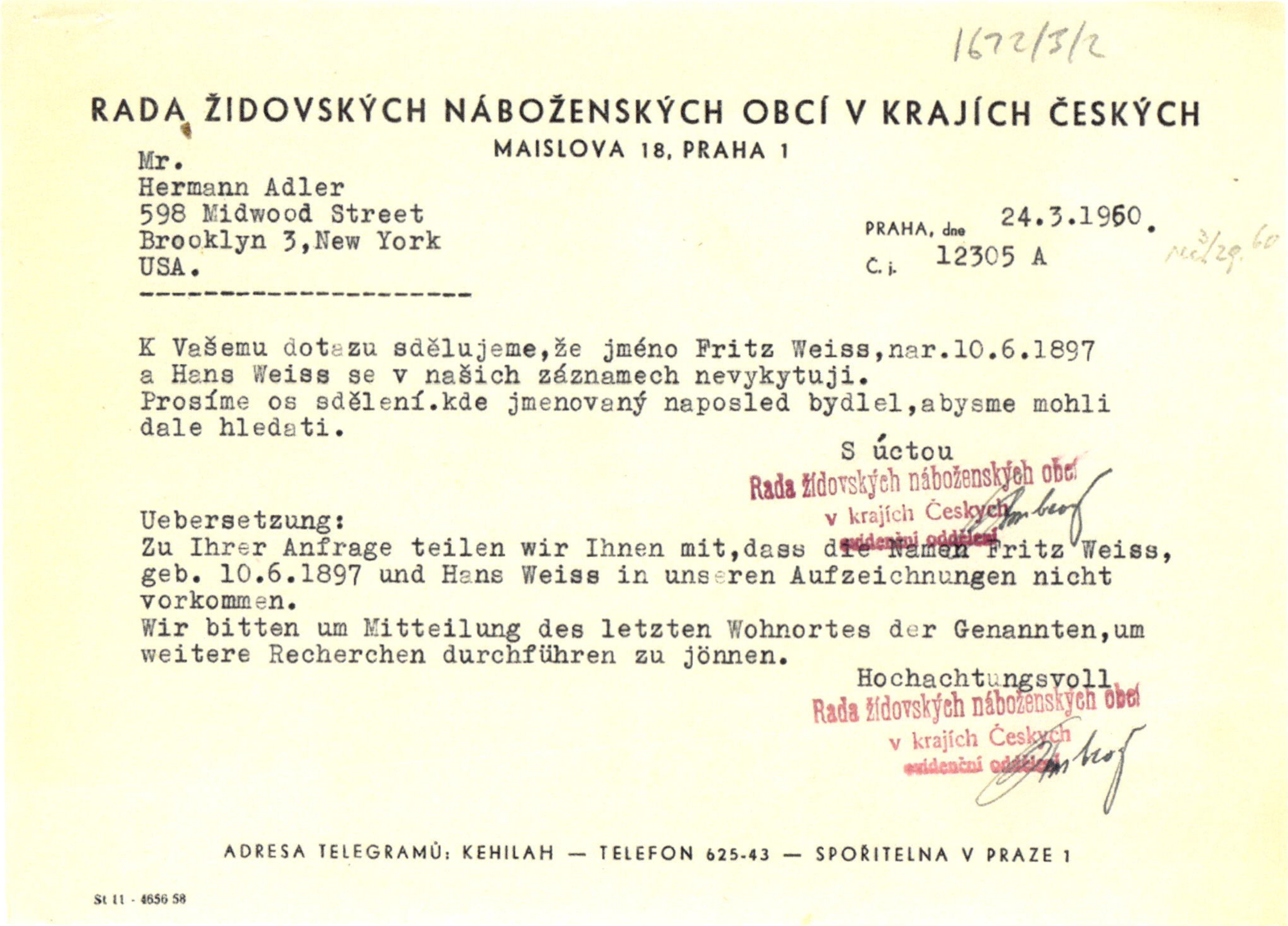

RADA ŽIDOVSKÝCH NÁBOŽENSKÝCH OBCÍ V KRAJÍCH ČESKÝCH
MAISLOVA 18, PRAHA 1

Mr.
Hermann Adler
598 Midwood Street
Brooklyn 3, New York
USA

PRAHA, dne 24.3.1960.
C.j. 12305 A

K Vašemu dotazu sdělujeme, že jméno Fritz Weiss, nar. 10.6.1897 a Hans Weiss se v našich záznamech nevykytují.
Prosíme os sdělení, kde jmenovaný naposled bydlel, abysme mohli dale hledati.

S úctou

Uebersetzung:
Zu Ihrer Anfrage teilen wir Ihnen mit, dass die Namen Fritz Weiss, geb. 10.6.1897 und Hans Weiss in unseren Aufzeichnungen nicht vorkommen.
Wir bitten um Mitteilung des letzten Wohnortes der Genannten, um weitere Recherchen durchführen zu jönnen.

Hochachtungsvoll

ADRESA TELEGRAMŮ: KEHILAH — TELEFON 625-43 — SPOŘITELNA V PRAZE 1

Adolf Adler (born in Vienna, 1895) and his wife Gisela emigrated to England in 1939. Adolf had been sent to Dachau in November 1938 and released. After the war, he began to investigate the whereabouts of his missing relatives. His correspondence reveals the multiple channels for researching missing fates.
© WL Collections

COMITÉ INTERNATIONAL DE LA CROIX-ROUGE
SERVICE INTERNATIONAL DE RECHERCHES
Arolsen (Waldeck) Allemagne

INTERNATIONAL TRACING SERVICE   INTERNATIONALER SUCHDIENST
Arolsen (Waldeck) Germany   Arolsen (Waldeck) Deutschland

Téléphone: Arolsen 434 · Télégrammes: ITS Arolsen

1674/5

Arolsen, den 17.August 1960

Mr.Herman Adler
598 Midwood Str.
Brooklyn 3
<u>NEW YORK</u>
N.Y.

Unser Zeichen   Ihr Zeichen   Ihr Schreiben vom
TD   8o7 411/412   7.5.1960

<u>Betrifft</u>: WEISS, Fritz, (Friedrich, Bedrich)?, geboren am 1o.6.1897
         in Goeding/Maehren,
         WEISS, Hans, geboren am 24.6.19o1 in Goeding/Maehren.

Sehr geehrter Herr Adler!

In Beantwortung Ihrer Suchanfrage teilen wir Ihnen mit, daß in den
Unterlagen des Internationalen Suchdienstes folgende Angaben enthalten sind:

   1.) WEISS, Bedrich, geboren am 1o.6.1897 in Kadonin,
       Staatsangehörigkeit: tschechoslowakisch, letzter
       Wohnort: 34, Bld Magenta,Paris oder 58 R d' Avron,Paris,
       wurde am 29.7.1942 vom Sammellager Drancy zum KL
       Auschwitz überstellt.- Weitere Angaben über den
       Verbleib des Gesuchten liegen nicht vor.
   2.) a WEIHS, Hans Viktor, letzter Wohnort: Wien XIV,
         Bujattig.3/1, (nähere Personalangaben fehlen),wurde am 23.1o.1941 mit dem 8.Transport (zusammen mit
         Weihs Charlotte) durch die Gestapo nach Lodz evakuiert.
       b WEISS, Hans, letzter Wohnort: Wien III, Gen.Krausspl.3
         (keine weiteren Personalangaben) mit dem 1o.Transport
         am 2.11.1941 durch die Gestapo nach Lodz evakuiert.

Infolge der unvollständigen Personalangaben können wir nicht feststellen,
ob einer dieser letzten Berichte auf den Gesuchten zutrifft.

                                    Hochachtungsvoll
                                    Im Auftrag:

                                    A. Opitz

Pl/Du.

Gathering the names

Tracing bureaus collected documentation related to the last known whereabouts of individuals. Material evidence not destroyed by the Germans, such as documents from concentration camps, hospitals and factories was repurposed for tracing work. To this were added Displaced Persons registration records and census lists compiled by different organisations, like the World Jewish Congress. Mass broadcasts over radio issued immediately after the war were another method for locating individuals.

Surviving documents were not always accurate or complete. Many victims and survivors shared the same name or spelt their name in numerous variations. Moreover, many had given false names and ages upon entering the camps or to liberating authorities.

Collecting documentation and facilitating field searches were two major logistical challenges. After the zonal offices were dissolved in the early 1950s, the focus shifted to searching for individuals based on the documents collected.

Gita Esther Nussbaum was born in Liepāja (then Lißau), Latvia on 2 March 1933. From about 1936, she was in the care of her aunt and uncle, Sophie and Noah Heiden, in Liepāja. After the war, her parents, who had survived with her older sister in Corsica, searched for her. Gita's fate is unknown, although she was most likely murdered in Liepāja in 1941.

© Courtesy Maurice Smith

While fielding tracing requests, the Central Tracing Bureau indexed the documents that were being collected for names. It also incorporated name index cards that had been created by other agencies, for example, by SHAEF to register Displaced Persons. The *Master Index*, known today as the *Central Names Index*, includes records of enquiries, summaries of search files, and references to documents. An alphabetic-phonetic filing system was instituted in 1949, which helped the ITS deal with spelling variants.

Central Names Index (CNI).
© International Tracing Service, Cornelis Gollhardt

These images demonstrate attempts to create a more formal work flow for fielding tracing requests. However, the process of actual tracing was far more complex.

Here, incoming mail is sorted according to language and country, in preparation for the search for the missing person.

Hoechst, Germany
c. 1945–48
© United Nations Archives

Multiple languages were needed to process requests for information. Often Displaced Persons were employed to help facilitate requests.

Hoechst, Germany
c. 1944–1948
© United Nations Archives

From July 1947, the Central Tracing Bureau was managed by the International Refugee Organization, which had been founded in 1946 and assumed most of the functions of its predecessor, UNRRA.

Excerpt from IRO: *What it is...what it does...how it works,* 1949.
© WL Collections

The Answer: NEW HOMES

The refugees cannot stay where they are. They don't want to live among their ex-enemies nor could they support themselves if settled in the shattered economies of these overcrowded lands. Homes, opportunities to work and to live anew, in countries all over the world, must be found for them.

❶ This refugee family is making the best of it in a shabby room in Germany, sustained chiefly by hope for the future.

❷ The first move in the voyage to a new land. These lucky ones leave a truck to board a train in Germany.

❸ Rugged young Lithuanians on their way to Canada. Later on, many will send for relatives left behind in refugee camps.

❹ Children waving goodbye to Germany and their refugee past. New homes, a new chance are ahead of them.

❺ A family of four boards an IRO vessel about to leave for Latin America.

❻ These nomads are near the end of their long road as they step from an IRO ship to friendly, welcoming soil.

In the context of the early Cold War, the Western Allies' decision to hand over the running of the Central Tracing Bureau to the IRO angered the Soviets. They objected to the IRO permitting people they claimed as Soviet citizens being allowed to resettle in Western countries on political grounds.

Files related to individuals applying to the IRO for assistance include many Eastern Europeans who wanted to resettle overseas rather than return to their countries of origin. This prompted the Soviets to withdraw their cooperation from centralised tracing.

This UN Displaced Persons identity card was issued to Iwan Demjanjuk, who did not wish to return to the Soviet Union for 'political and religious reasons.' After emigrating to the United States, he was later accused and convicted as an accessory to the murder of nearly 30,000 Jews in Sobibor death camp, where he worked as a guard.
© WL ITS Digital Archive 66866153

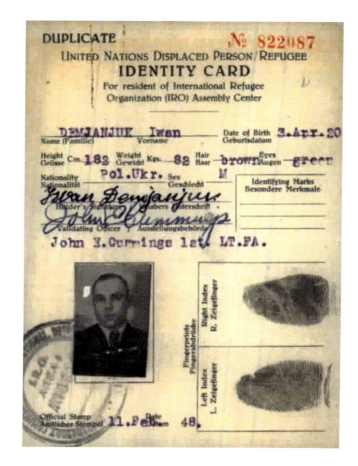

DEM SONDERSTANDESAMT VORGELEGT	Datum:

Name: SCHWARTZ, Jolan   B= 11415
geboren am 18.11.1922 in .... Nat. Ungarn/Jüdin
gestorben am 11.9.1944, 18"15 in Gelsenkirchen
Todesursache: Tod durch Fliegerangriff
beerdigt am .... in ....

STERBEURKUNDE Nr. 300 am. Bm. (Stempel) Datum 11.6.58
ausgestellt aufgrund folgender Dokumente:

bitte wenden

In 1949, the Bonn government opened a *Sonderstandesamt* (special register office) in Arolsen, which issued death certificates. These were used to expedite the restitution process. If the new office gave the new West German state the imprimatur of sovereignty – a cause of concern for some – it also embedded the West German commitment to the International Tracing Service.

Death certificate for Jolan Schwartz.
© WL ITS Digital Archive 43540431

On 4 August 1955, Nicholas Burkhardt wrote to Alfred Wiener, the founder of The Wiener Library, about his appointment as the head of the International Tracing Service. Wiener maintained frequent contact with the ITS, particularly regarding research on the Library's eyewitness accounts and to obtain copies of the ITS's publications.
© WL Collections

COMITÉ INTERNATIONAL DE LA CROIX-ROUGE
SERVICE INTERNATIONAL DE RECHERCHES
Arolsen
(Waldeck - Allemagne)

INTERNATIONAL TRACING SERVICE	INTERNATIONALER SUCHDIENST
Arolsen	Arolsen
(Waldeck - Germany)	(Waldeck - Deutschland)

Téléphone: Arolsen 434 · Câbles, télégrammes: ITS Arolsen

August 4, 1955

Dear Sir:

May I kindly draw your attention to the Agreement concluded on June 6, 1955 between the International Commission for the International Tracing Service and the International Committee of the Red Cross, concerning the future administration and direction of the International Tracing Service at Arolsen.

I have the honour to inform you that the International Committee of the Red Cross has nominated me for the position of Director of the International Tracing Service and that on July 22, 1955 the International Commission for the International Tracing Service unanimously agreed to my nomination.

I, therefore, assumed the directorship of the International Tracing Service on July 25, 1955. Mr. C.L. Widger, the former Interim Director, will remain with me temporarily as Assistant Director.

Sincerely yours,

N. Burckhardt
Director

The Wiener Library
19 Manchester Square,
London W. 1.

Identifying the unknown dead

The Allied authorities issued an order in October 1945 to all mayors across Germany 'to discover, register and eventually concentrate into separate national cemeteries, all Allied graves'. Fieldworkers set out to check graves and retrace the steps of concentration camp inmates who had been sent on forced marches (often called 'death marches').

Fieldworkers compiled summaries and hand-drawn maps identifying the location of 'unknown dead' and grave sites. They collected witness statements from those who saw the death marches. These investigations continued until 1951.

The investigations formed part of the materials the CTB (later the International Tracing Service) used to trace missing persons.

Establishing the death of an individual had legal repercussions. Some missing persons had property and assets to which their heirs were entitled. Widows could not remarry and orphans could not be adopted until the death of spouses or parents were confirmed.

In April 1950, the United Nations Convention on the Declaration of Death of Missing Persons established a procedure to obtain a declaration of death for missing persons.

Moses Liss, his wife, Laja, and their son David were deported in October 1938 from Gleiwitz (then Germany) to Poland. They remained in Warsaw, from where they managed to send David to Belfast on a Kindertransport. The last letters David received from his parents were dated from 1942. ITS documents reveal that Moses Liss was deported to Gross-Rosen, transferred to Flossenbürg and then Buchenwald. An Allied investigation identified the body of Liss by his Flossenbürg prisoner number. He was eventually reburied in a grave in Neunburg.

ONE MACAULAY COURT
LONDON S.W.4.
MAC. 6530

May 2nd, 1955.

Dear Sirs,

The MANCHESTER GUARDIAN has just published an article on your work which is of interest to me as I have never been able to establish the ultimate fate of my parents.

I quote below all I remember of their personal particulars and should be very grateful if you would try to trace them in your records.

	Father	Mother
Born at	Włodisław, Poland	Warsaw
on	15-3-1893	10-7-1896
Names	Moszek (or Moritz) Liss or Lis	Laja (or Lotte), née Mendelson
Resident on 1-9-39 at	Ulica Ogrodowa 35 m. 37, Warsaw.	

T-169 576
T-169 577

..../2

- 2 -

They were still alive and in Warsaw early in 1942, because they answered Red Cross messages I sent to the above address. In one message they mentioned that they had work; my father having been a tailor by profession this would seem to indicate that he worked in one of the uniform factories which I believe were established in the Warsaw ghetto. The last message I had was dated somewhere between May and July 1942.

The double spelling of the surname I quoted on the first page is explained by the fact that they lived in Gleiwitz, Upper Silesia, Germany, for years; however, they returned to Poland in the autumn of 1938, at the time of the forced repatriation of some thousands of Polish Jews.

If there is anything at all you can tell me about them, I shall be glad to hear from you.

Yours sincerely,

David Liss.

The International Tracing Service,
Arolsen near Kassel,
Germany.

ATTEMPTED IDENTIFICATION

6833	?	+ 28640 or (128640)	Buchenwald: WACHSMANN, Salomon – Pol. Jew
11565	?	32563	Flossenbürg: GURIN, Sergej – Russ.
14566 or 114566	Buchenwald: CUBIZOLLE, Louis – French / Flossenbürg: FIRGENZWEIG, Motek – Polish Jew	57663	Buchenwald: WIRTHEIM, Salomon – Hung. Jew.
19226 or 19266	Buchenwald: MALYSCHOK, Andrej – Russ.	64564	?
20018	?	P 82310	Flossenbürg: KLÜGER, Elias – Polish Jew
L 27381 or (127381)	Buchenwald: SPIEWAK, Dawid – Polish Jew	P 82396	Flossenbürg: LIS, Moses – Polish Jew

An American soldier studies a grave marker on the sight of a mass grave of death march victims. The ITS made the investigation of death march routes a central focus of its work in 1951.

c. 1945
© USHMM, courtesy of Joseph Eaton

A clandestine photograph of prisoners marching to Dachau on a death march. Maria Seidenberger took this photo from the window of her family's home. According to Czech political prisoner, Karel Kasak, pictured among the inmates, the prisoners were coming from Nuremberg.

26 April 1945.
© USHMM, courtesy of Maria Seidenberger

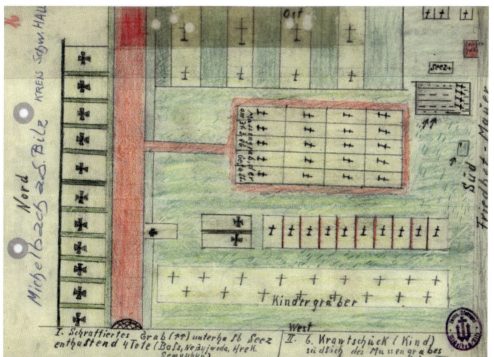

This map of a grave in Michelbach an der Bilz (Baden-Württemberg) was drawn as part of the ITS's post-war investigations of burial sites in occupied Germany. Investigations of grave sites helped reconstruct the history of the death marches. Notes on the map indicate the burial places of individuals with the surnames Seez, Bass, Nessyjwoda, Hrek, Semyschyn, and a child named Krawtschück. There is also a mass grave identified in the center.
© WL ITS Digital archive, 101099771

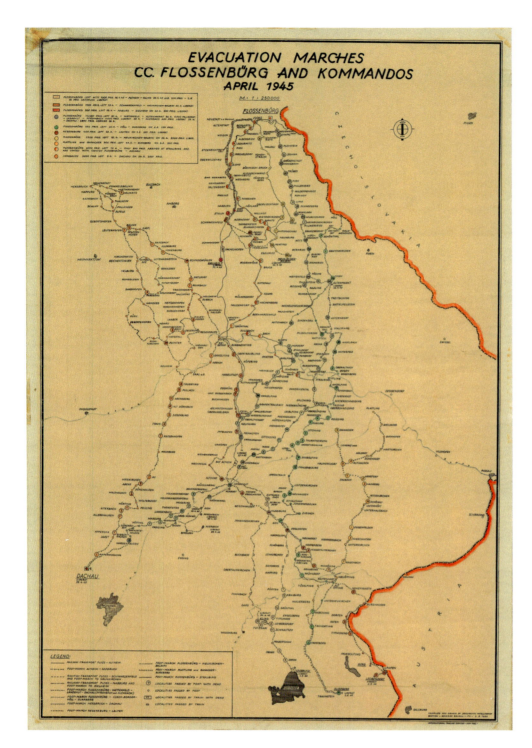

Investigations relied on field operations, burial site searches, grave identifications, questioning of mayors, examination of hospital records and interviews with survivors in Displaced Persons camps. Based on these investigations, the ITS created maps showing the routes of the death marches, for example, this map detailing those from the Flossenbürg camp. Due to a lack of resources, the investigations ended in 1951.

Evacuation Marches CC Flossenbürg and Kommandos (IV-5-E), April 1945, 10.12.694
© ITS Bad Arolsen.

THE GERMAN CONCENTRATION CAMPS

1. General

This publication represents an attempt to compile the names, locations and pertinent data of confirmed, reported, or alleged detention centres in Axis Europe which come within the elastic definition "Concentration Camp". "Elastic" because there are many types of detention camps used by the Germans in addition to the official Konzentrationslager (Concentration Camps). Among these are:-

Arbeitslager (Work Camps)
Zwangslager (Forcible Detention Camps)
Zwangsarbeitslager (Penal Servitude Camps)
Zivilgefangenenlager (Detention Camps for Civilians)
Straflager (Punitive Camps)

Various preparations, made by camp officials, have been reported in case of an Allied invasion of Germany proper. Stores of poison gas are said to be kept at some camps and inmates have been threatened that they would be shot or poisoned immediately upon the arrival of Allied troops. SS Officers are said to have civilian clothes hidden under their beds. For the camp at VUGHT, at least, it has been reported that the Commander intends to turn over the camp to inmates supposed to be members of the former Communist Party of the Netherlands in order to create turmoil and prevent records and men from falling into Allied hands.

If the evacuation of NATZWEILER Concentration Camp is taken as an example, however, the above reports would appear false. With the rapid Allied advance, after the initial battles in France, preparations were made by the Germans for the evacuation of the camp and all its Aussenlager (Subsidiary Labour Camps). These movements were successfully carried out, thus allowing the Germans to retain much-needed manpower and machinery and denying this, along with possible sources of information, to the Allies.

It should be remembered that concentration camps, in addition to providing a social and political problem, may also furnish a considerable number of Germans well disposed towards the Allies.

2. Definition of a Concentration Camp

According to German law, a Konzentrationslager (officially abbreviated to KL, but popularly referred to as KZ) provides Schutzhaft (Protective Custody) for persons who have not been legally sentenced to imprisonment by a court of law, and/or those who, having served a legal sentence, have been ordered further detention by the Gestapo (Secret State Police), Sicherheitsdienst (SD – Security Service) or the Geheime Feldpolizei (Secret Field Police).

Due to the scarcity of documentary evidence, which is only slowly becoming available, the indefinite nature of details obtained from former inmates and the similarity in administration and treatment of charges at these various types of detention centre, many camps have been incorrectly reported as Konzentrationslager, although they are actually different types of establishments.

From recent reports, it appears that only fourteen camps in greater Germany, are centrally administered by the WVHA (see para 9). All other camps are Aussenlager (Subsidiary Camps) of these fourteen.

The centrally administered camps are:-

AUSCHWITZ	MAUTHAUSEN
BUCHENWALD	NATZWEILER
DACHAU	NIEDERHAGEN
FLOSSENBURG	NEUENGAMME
GROSS ROSEN	RAVENSBRÜCK
HERZOGENBUSCH	SACHSENHAUSEN
HINZERT	STUTTHOF

(Sonderlager für Eindeutschungsfähige, or Special Camp for persons eligible for Germanisation)

Reports are often vague concerning the true status of many camps, being almost invariably incomplete, based on hearsay, mutilated in transmission, distorted in some fashion or out of date.

Legal definitions for the camps differ widely in the various German-occupied areas of Europe. For example, Straflager (Punitive Camps) in Poland are frequently somewhat similar to prisons, and serve the same purpose, but the treatment of inmates may correspond to that practised in concentration camps in Germany.

There appears to be no definite formula for the establishment of detention centres. New camps are often attached to existing penal institutions, or a Konzentrationslager may be added to or use the facilities of a Zuchthaus (Penitentiary) (the KL ORANIENBURG uses the crematorium at the PLÖTZENSEE Zuchthaus).

Concentration Camps may be expanded by the addition, for example, of a Straflager für Arbeitsverweigerer (Penal Camp for Persons Refusing to Work).

PW Dulags (Durchgangslager, or Transit Camps) and internment camps have appeared erroneously in some lists as KLs, perhaps because the term Dulag may also be applied to collecting stations of all sorts for Schutzhäftlinge (Persons in Protective Custody). The Dulags mentioned in the list (Annexe A, Part Two), however, are most likely for Schutzhäftlinge and in no way connected with those of the armed forces of Germany, and deserve, therefore, to be incorporated.

Regular Wehrmacht penal establishments are referred to as Soldatenkonzentrationslager (SKs or Soldiers' Concentration Camps) or Sonder KZs (Special Purpose Concentration Camps).

3. Grading of Prisoners

According to a document of September 1940, inmates were specially graded by the RFSS u Ch d Dt Pol for commitment to different types of camps.

Stufe 1 (Grade 1) – For all persons under light sentence and corrigibles; also, for cases of solitary confinement and other special cases.(DACHAU and SACHSENHAUSEN).

Stufe 1a (Grade 1a) – For all aged persons and those of limited work ability, but who can still be employed in vegetable gardening (DACHAU).

Investigations into the 'death marches' and their routes were aided by the collection of other documentation from the camps as well as eye-witness testimonies. This document was compiled by the US Secret Service with the aid of émigrés from Nazi-occupied Europe. It shows remarkable early knowledge of the camp system and the network of subcamps across the Reich.

Basic Handbook KLs (Konzentrationslager): Axis Concentration Camps and Detention Centres Reported as such in Europe, SHAEF, c. 1944–45.
© WL ITS Digital Archive 82328575

'In the best interests of the child'

Tens of thousands of children became separated from their parents or orphaned by the end of the Second World War. Approximately 150,000 Jewish youth survived in liberated Europe.

Among the children who found themselves alone at war's end were those who had survived concentration camps and children of foreign forced labourers. Parents searched for children who had been kidnapped by German authorities because they had been considered 'racially suitable' and 'Germanised'.

The Child Search Branch was a special office of the International Tracing Service. It launched the Limited Registration Plan, a programme to check German foster homes, orphanages, hospitals and local records for missing children. Bereft parents submitted tracing requests, which were handled by the Child Tracing Section.

Through its field work, the ITS identified thousands of children who, in their opinion, belonged somewhere else, usually with their biological parents. The decision to remove a child from foster care was not easy and fraught with ethical and emotional challenges.

The wishes of the children did not always match those of their carers. Many children were too young to be able to tell aid workers who they were, or could no longer recall their lives before the war. Some had grown attached to their foster parents and did not wish to return to their biological families. Some children dreamed of joining the *Bricha*, the underground effort to help Jewish survivors escape post-war Europe for Mandate Palestine.

'Six years in Germany is a long time in the life of a child, especially when he is taught to forget his past to learn new ways.'
Jean Henshaw, UNRRA in the Role of Foster Parent, 1946

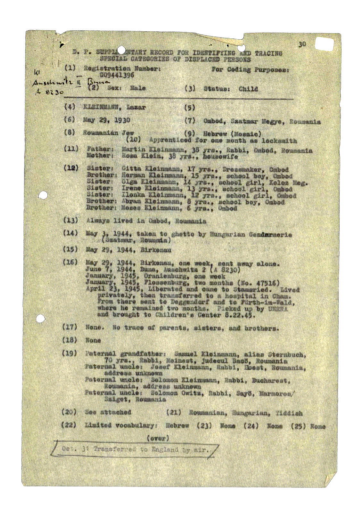
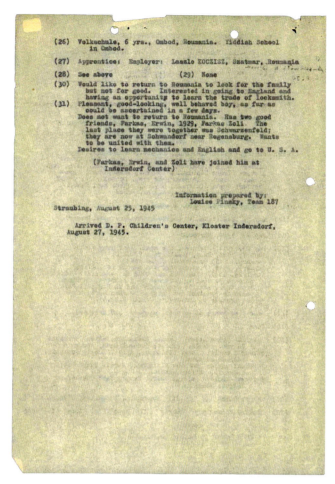

Lázár Kleinman was born on 29 May 1929 in Ambud, a small village near Satu Mare, Romania, into an Orthodox Jewish family of eight children. After Hungary occupied northern Transylvania in 1940, his family's life was brutally upended. In 1944, his father was deported and he and his family were put into a ghetto. From there they were deported to Auschwitz-Birkenau. After surviving several camps, Kleinman was found by UNRRA after the war and placed in the Kloster Indersdorf children's home. Leslie was taken to England on a special transport in 1946. He continues to speak about his experiences to audiences throughout the UK.

© WL ITS Digital Archive, 84313461, 84313464_01-02

<u>Translation</u>

Lodz, 29.10.1947.

My dear child!

I have been informed by Office that you are living at Mr. Kastner's and that many Polish children forgot that they are Poles and they do not want to return. My dear Natalik, you were going to Polish school and you were old enough to remember when you were taken by Germans and when they sent Poles to Germany as workers. Now all are coming back and you must do the same because you are a Polish child. You will return not only to your mother but to your own country whose bread you ate. Now when the war is over your place is in Poland. I was told you do not want to return ? You are wounding my heart! Perhaps, your foster-mother has no children and if she has, she can explain to you what is mother's heart pain. You are the child of a mother-Pole and you were not bred for a foreign country by me. If your foster-mother did not let you go, God should punish her, I shall say my prayer to Virgin Mary for it.

Do you know, I have still the same picture of Virgin Mary of Crestochava which you had in you childhood. Did you receive the doll I sent you some time from Germany ?

I end and I ask you to remember:

> You were born from Polish soil
> We are bred on Polish soil
> We are fed by Polish soil

and it will receive us back.

Your mother Kazimiera Skibinska

I kiss you heartily. Be healthy and write at once.

Translated by K. Kaminski.

In 1947, Kazimiera Skibińska pleaded with her daughter, Natalia (b. 1932), to return to Poland after the war. The Child Search Branch had found Natalia, who had been raised by a German family after her mother, who came to Germany as a labourer, placed her in a children's home. Natalia refused to return, despite her mother's anguished letters.

© WL ITS Digital Archive, 84504500

Ludwig Stein (Gasparik)

A Czech boy of 15, Ludwig described his harrowing experiences to relief workers after the war. His parents had both been interned in Buchenwald and died. He was desperate to emigrate to the United States where he had relatives.

Ludwig's case file reveals his fragile emotional state. The relief workers cared for him with difficulty and their resources were stretched. It turned out that Ludwig falsified his wartime story. He claimed to be Jewish so that he could get help to go to the United States. According to postwar testimony, Ludwig managed to get to Italy with IRO aid and then on to Palestine.

While children may have altered their biographical details to meet IRO rules, the majority of child cases were not fabricated. Ludwig Gasparik's case reveals the psychological impact of war on children. It also shows the IRO review board's complex, imperfect process of evaluation. The IRO's determination of 'eligibility' often directed the fates of children.

© WL ITS Digital Archive, 84519736, 84519733

Translation.

Jewish Agency for Palestine
Branch Office Vienna III,
16, Marokkanergasse.

C o p y.

A lady travelling to Erez and on passage here gave me your esteemed address saying that you are very helpful and so I too hope to have found the right address for my request.

My case is as follows:

My only child, a girl 6 years old, has been abducted by the Germans in 1944 and the only thing I know is that the child is said to have been in Camp Birkenau. My husband, who had been in the same camp, came back again on 20th October, 1945, but there was no trace left of the child, please note that the child had been in the same camp. As my child was a particularly beautiful child, very strong and healthy, it might be that my child is among the surviving children. Now I have heard that Joint had started sort of an action in order to trace Jewish children living with Aryans in Poland and to ransom them. Besides, many of the surviving children are said to be living in Austria and Germany.

My request to you, much esteemed Mr. Mantel, is, whether you could not undertake something in my matter or advise me what I should do in order to find my beloved only child again.

I know, dear sir, that you receive many such letters, but I should not have written to you if you would not have been described to me as such a really good and helpful man, who will understand an unhappy mother.

The child's name is Susi Talvi born 18.11.1937. In order to cover her Jewish name, we called her Sula during the last time. It might be that the child remembers this name. I am attaching an old photograph, it might be that the child remembers her mother when she is shown this picture.

My address is: Athens, Vassilis Sophia 4, Mme Sarah Talvi.

I hope that I have not requested in vain and beseech you to answer me quickly and thank you very much

sgd. Zara Talvi.

IP 17.11.48.

Translation.

Have pity on me, an unhappy mother, for the Nazis (those ferocious beasts) took away my little daughter, the only child I had.
I pray you with all my soul to trace my little daughter among the children saved. My little daughter is called Suzy Talvi, born 18th November, 1937, in Athens, deported from Athens to Birkenau on 20th June, 1944. Her father has been saved from Birkenau and is called Mair, and I, the mother, am called Sara.

The photo had been taken in 1940.

IP 17.11.1948.

On 17 November 1948, Sara Talvi wrote to the Tracing Bureau about 'the only child' she had. Suzy Talvi was born on 18 November 1937 in Athens, from where she was deported to Auschwitz-Birkenau in June 1944. The last communication in Suzy Talvi's Child Search case file is dated December 1953.

© WL ITS Digital Archive 84594484, 84594493, 84594494

Legacies of Fates Known and Unknown

The search for the millions of people who went missing after the Second World War continues today. Institutions such as The Wiener Library, the International Tracing Service (Germany), the US Holocaust Memorial Museum (USA) and Yad Vashem (Israel) help people discover the fates of their relatives by navigating through documents and other traces of evidence left behind.

Today, refugees, migrants and others searching for missing family members can turn to the International Committee of the Red Cross and Red Crescent Societies, among other organisations. The ICRC and Red Crescent Societies in Europe have created a website, *Trace the Face*, where individuals can upload images and reconnect with family members (familylinks.icrc.org). REFUNITE (refunite.org) is a non-profit organisation that helps forcibly displaced people find missing family members.

Documentary evidence of persecution, where it exists, assists with claims for compensation, stolen property and other assets. Yet scattered records around the world mean that a search can take months, years and decades. In many cases, no relatives or descendants remained alive to carry on a search for the missing. Entire communities were destroyed.

These stories remain untold.

When someone goes missing the threads that connect our stories and our lives are strained, even broken. The loss of someone we love shows us something about who we are, and how closely we are bound to each other. Indeed, it shows us that who we are comes in large part from our ties to others.

Jenny Edkins, *Missing* (2011)

Searching at the Wiener Library

The Wiener Library helps visitors find information on the fates of their loved ones using the UK's digital copy of the International Tracing Service (ITS) archive and other records in its collections. In rare cases, relatives are reunited or find descendants they never knew existed.

The ITS archive contains some 30 million documents on over 17.5 million people. Yet it is only a fragment of the entire documentary record on the persecution of Jews and other victims during the Holocaust.

To learn how to begin your search, visit our website: wienerlibrary.co.uk/ITS.

The Central Names Index in Bad Arolsen, Germany.
© Cornelius Gollhardt

"This vast collection of documented horror preserves the patches, the fragments, the detritus of...17 million lives on 47 million pieces of paper." Daša Drndić, *Trieste* (2011)

© Richard Ehrlich, US Holocaust Memorial Museum

In 1963, the ITS received over 4,000 personal items that had been recovered from liberated German prisons and camps, including Neuengamme, Dachau, Natzweiler and Bergen-Belsen. The ITS now actively seeks to return the objects to their original owners or descendants. The objects are of little material value, but hold great emotional significance. Learn more by visiting its-arolsen.org and following #StolenMemory.

© International Tracing Service, Bad Arolsen

Responses to the Wiener Library's Family Research

I think what I am already finding difficult, and this is a sentiment which I must share with others, is bringing into my consciousness the realities as they affected my family personally and not as just 1 in 6 million. I understand that to many people it's 'just another story', a story like many others, with different paths and, sadly different destinations, but it is one of the stories which make up the whole. How I will feel at the end and how I will tell it to my children I do not yet know. Thank you again for starting me off on something I should have tackled years ago but could not.

I am just beginning to adjust to the facts that you revealed to me. It takes time as you said. I am glad I finally know definitively what happened to her but somehow that is difficult too. In one way it was easier when it wasn't quite so certain. As someone who generally prefers to know what is going on however awful, these ambivalent feelings help me to have more insight and sympathy towards those who prefer not to know.

A big thank you for all your hard work and diligence. Although we will probably never find out the exact circumstances of my aunt's fate I do feel as much has been done as possible.

I am completely overwhelmed by your comprehensive response to my enquiry. Whilst I knew the bare outline of my grandparents' 'journey to extinction', you have filled in many invaluable details. It grieves me a bit that I was unable to find out this information before my mother's death in 2011 - she would have had a likely actual 'yahrzeit' to commemorate, the lack of which distressed her immeasurably. Your meticulous research is so appreciated.

My mother is thrilled to find a lot of this information out from you, given my grandfather was not keen to talk about his terrible experiences whilst he was alive. I've been working on trying to piece together my grandfather's life each night over the past week or so, and am starting to get a better feel for what my grandfather went through.

Thank you so much for all the interesting documents you have sent me. I never dreamed I would see them with my own eyes. While you are correct in saying I am familiar with most of the contents, still, reading the precision with which the Nazis recorded our fate as well as everybody else's sends shivers down my spine. Also, I am so happy to have dates of our various transports, for those I had to rely on the memory of friends.

A Family reunion across time and space

In October 2017, Michael Pollak from Australia contacted The Wiener Library. He was searching for information on his grandfather, Hans Friedmann. Research in the International Tracing Service digital archive revealed a number of documents connected with Hans, his arrest in Germany as part of the November Pogrom (*Kristallnacht*), and his three-month incarceration in Buchenwald concentration camp.

After his release on 26 January 1939, Hans emigrated to the UK. There he was interned in the Kitchener camp before serving in the Royal Pioneer Corps and then the British Army. During his service, he changed his name to Joe Freedman.

Included among Joe's documents was his Tracing and Documentation file – evidence of searches for him conducted since the end of the war. One page of the file mentioned a wife. From this clue, the Library found documents related to his wife Lydia and their son Alfred, both of whom had remained in Germany after Joe (then, Hans) left for the UK. The research revealed that both Lydia and Alfred were deported from Frankfurt to Minsk on 11 November 1941, where both perished.

The documents also showed that Lydia had several siblings. Two of her sisters, Herta and Edith, both survived the Holocaust and contacted the ITS after the war to search for their lost sister. Armed with this information, Michael has been able to trace and make contact with Edith's grandchildren:

'Incredibly, I managed to find a phone number for Edith's grand-daughter in the US and had a lengthy chat with her and exchanged emails and even photos of Alfred and Lydia with her … I've also now spoken to Edith's son Sidney … and last night, I actually spoke to Herta's only child, Ruthie.'

Lydia and her sisters and mother.
© Michael Pollak

Hans (Joe) with his first wife, Lydia.

Lydia with Alfred. Both were deported from Frankfurt to Minsk in 1941. There they were murdered.

Hans (Joe), with his second wife Charlotte on their wedding day in October 1946.

Michael Pollak (second from left) with his mother (second from right), Sue. Sue was Hans'/Joe's daughter from his second marriage to Charlotte.

This excerpt from a Tracing and Documentation file includes a form in which Hans mentioned his wife Lydia.

© WL ITS Digital Archive, 100686702

Anlage zur Veränderungs-
meldung vom 25.Jan.1939. K.L.Buchenwald, den 25.Januar 1939.

Namentliche Liste der am 25.Januar 1939 entlassenen
Aktions - Juden.

Lfd.Nr.	Häftl.Nr.	Name
1	29589	Appel, Leopold
2	21924	Frenkel, Max
3	29550	Friedmann, Hans
4	26513	Goldsand, Löwi
5	26602	Goldschmidt, Walter
6	24873	Herz, Herbert
7	29456	Herz, Manfred
8	25052	Hess, Ernst
9	24840	Hirsch, Alfred
10	29266	Horowitz, Karl
11	21598	Joskowicz, Israel
12	29379	Kahn, Alfred
13	26639	Kahn II, Gustav
14	29349	Katz, Alfred
15	21569	Kirschner, Siegfried
16	21617	Levi, Richard
17	21478	Levita, Ernst
18	29921	Levy, Siegfried
19	24317	Lewin, Abram
20	25505	Lichtenstein, Norbert
21	29884	Lichtenstein, Sigmund
22	25818	Lion, Leopold
23	24819	Loeb, Julius
24	26226	Mansbach, Bernhard
25	30599	May, Heinrich
26	25374	Mayer, Alfred
27	26535	Melitz, Bruno
28	29846	Meyer, Leonhard
29	21793	Mondschein, René
30	26304	Oettinger, Manfred
31	25921	Rapp, Karl
32	26051	Rosenberg, Heinz
33	25691	Rotschild, Julius
34	24911	Salomon, Dr. Rudolf
35	25099	Selig, Berthold
36	30174	Sondheim, Eugen
37	21577	Speyer, Adolf
38	29427	Schwarz, Karl
39	29286	Stein, Ludwig
40	26682	Stern, Herbert
41	30088	Stiefel, Helmut
42	26786	Strauss, Max
43	21559	Wachtelkönig, Markus
44	25082	Weiss, Ernst
45	25080	Weissmann, Max
46	29588	Winter, Karl
47	21480	Wolff, Bruno
48	29674	Würzburger, Paul
49	30103	Zylberstein, Chaim

0011451

Hans Friedmann appeared on a list of Jews released from Buchenwald on 25 January 1939.
© WL ITS Digital Archive, 5728399

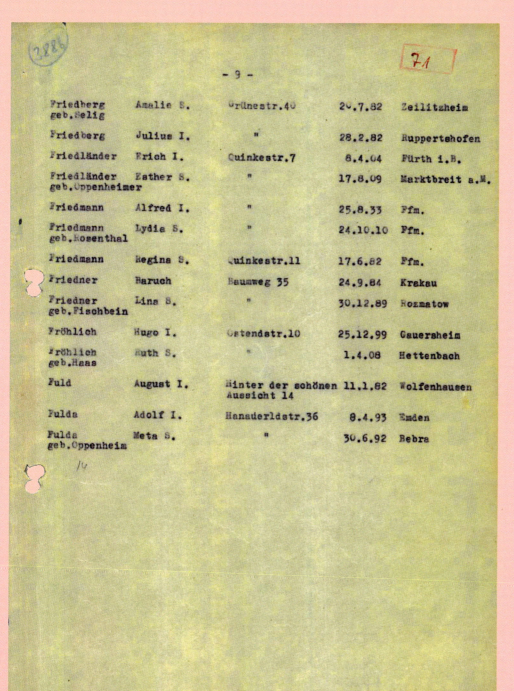

Lydia and her son, Alfred, appeared on a transport list to Minsk, dated 11 November 1941.
© WL ITS Digital Archive, 11199992

- 9 -

Friedberg geb.Selig	Amalie S.	Grünestr.40	20.7.82	Zeilitzheim
Friedberg	Julius I.	"	28.2.82	Ruppertshofen
Friedländer	Erich I.	Quinkestr.7	8.4.04	Fürth i.B.
Friedländer geb.Oppenheimer	Esther S.	"	17.8.09	Marktbreit a.M.
Friedmann	Alfred I.	"	25.8.33	Ffm.
Friedmann geb.Rosenthal	Lydia S.	"	24.10.10	Ffm.
Friedmann	Regina S.	Quinkestr.11	17.6.82	Ffm.
Friedner	Baruch	Baumweg 35	24.9.84	Krakau
Friedner geb.Fischbein	Lina S.	"	30.12.89	Rozmatow
Fröhlich	Hugo I.	Ostendstr.10	25.12.99	Gauersheim
Fröhlich geb.Haas	Ruth S.	"	1.4.08	Hettenbach
Fuld	August I.	Hinter der schönen Aussicht 14	11.1.82	Wolfenhausen
Fulda	Adolf I.	Hanauerldstr.36	8.4.93	Emden
Fulda geb.Oppenheim	Meta S.	"	30.6.92	Bebra

Epilogue
by Professor Dan Stone

When the International Tracing Service was created in 1948, it did not emerge fully formed from the minds of Allied occupation authorities. Rather, the institution that appeared in Arolsen was created to coordinate the wide array of tracing agencies that had existed since the war. Numerous charities had established their own agencies, and the Red Cross was also using expertise gained over previous decades in seeking the missing, especially POWs. During the period of UNRRA control over the fledgling Central Tracing Bureau (1945–1947), the CTB was itself more of a clearing house for tracing work carried out by national and zonal tracing bureaus in occupied Germany, only becoming the main centre of operations after 1948. After about 1950, most of the documents acquired by charities such as the American Jewish Joint Distribution Committee and the Central Location Index (New York City) were handed over to ITS, which then became the centralised location for tracing.

The complex history of ITS reflects the chaotic situation at the end of the war. As early as November 1943, the Jewish Refugees Committee, for example, convened a meeting to discuss establishing a Centralised Search Bureau. Chaired by noted Anglo-Jewish campaigner Otto Schiff, the committee also comprised representatives of the Quakers, the British Red Cross Society, the Association of Jewish Refugees and the Women's Voluntary Services, among others. From the start the committee assumed that the Red Cross was the sole agency that could coordinate the work of the various bodies involved in tracing; they also assumed – wrongly – that the military would only deal with the problem cursorily and then, when they were willing to let charities into the liberated zones, leave it to them to handle.[1] The JRC's aim was to compile a list of German and Austrian refugees in Britain with relatives on the Continent, so that once UNRRA began its work of registering DPs it could match them with people in Britain looking for them.

One of the most fascinating of the early tracing offices was the functionally-named International Information Office (IIO), set up in Dachau after the liberation of the camp. It was founded on the basis of the camp registration office (*Lagerschreibstube*), which had existed in the camp since 1933. From November 1944, its head was Jan Domagała, who was assisted by several other fellow former inmates. As the war was coming to an end, they hid the camp records at considerable personal risk, and then, following the liberation, they ran the IIO, established in June 1945 on the orders of the US Military Government. Operating at first in the camp, it was soon relocated to the town of Dachau, and was very well staffed, with 'forty-two block writers, forty evidence writers, and twenty-nine office writers.'[2]

By the middle of 1946, former inmate Walter Cieslik had taken over as head of the IIO. One of the first things he did was to publish a report on the death marches from Dachau, whose aim, as he wrote, was 'to help the unfortunate families of those former prisoners of Dachau Concentration Camp, who were abducted to the mountain regions of South Bavaria a few days before the Camp was liberated by US Army.'[3] As with other early postwar tracing projects, Cieslik combined this explanation of the publication's purpose with an appeal:

> Hundreds of people are waiting the return of their relations, who never come back from Dachau Conc. Camp. The International Information Office has endeavoured to reveal the mystery of the many unknown graves by circular letters, inquiries, and by examination of various eye-witnesses.

By the present material may be shown how difficult it is, to obtain positive results. In the name of the widow's and orphan's tears for the murdered, we kindly beg everybody who is able to give directions concerning the contents of this book for informations about observations and worth knowing facts. All this can help to relieve the chance of so many unfortunate relations.[4]

Indeed, sometimes the inquiry process was lucky and family members could be reunited. Occasionally, this meant even more than one family member, as in this example from the ITS's *Monthly Report* for September 1949:

> In response to a newspaper publication, concerning an enquiry received from a father for his 13 years old son, he last heard of 1939, the following letter was received:
> 'You broadcast for missing persons [sic] I am living in Marburg/Lahn and married. We have two children and are awaiting the third. Would you please inform me, who is searching for me, in order to get in touch with this person.'
> The father had evidently forgotten that his son had grown older in intervening years, and as a result of Mass Tracing action he found not only his son but a daughter-in-law and two grandchildren.[5]

Even so, the IIO set the tone for ITS. Cieslik's realism has prevailed ever since, and for all the wealth of its documentary collections, tracing remains a hit and miss affair: millions of fates remain unknown. But ITS has never stopped trying to trace the missing and even today, as it is also becoming a research and commemoration institute, it receives about 1,000 tracing requests per month, with the Wiener Library, US Holocaust Memorial Museum and Yad Vashem adding many more to that number.

This is thus not a closed history but one that connects us to the world of the Nazi atrocities with immediacy, and sometimes shock. The documents in its immense archive allow us to follow the ITS as it uncovered facts and discovered people – and failed to do so. Today we can echo that process of discovery by using the sources to write fine-grained histories of little-known aspects of the Holocaust, such as the hundreds of sub-camps that pockmarked Europe in the late stages of the war. At the heart of both discovery processes – ITS's in its tracing work and ours in retracing ITS's steps today – lies a profound ethical promise:

> Doubtless we stand before a riddle, which is hard to solve, as a great part of the victims will never be found. But we don't doubt, that it is possible to us, by the collaboration of everybody who is able to assist us in this case, to answer the numerous inquiries for the fate and the graves of the unhappy victims, in writing to the concerned families. The human fellow-feeling demand to bury in a cemetery equal under equals all those who it was not granted to reach freedom. This are expecting thousands of families of the murdered victims and this is expecting human sympathy.[6]

1 Jewish Refugees Committee, *Minutes of Meeting to Discuss Establishment of Centralised Search Bureau, Held at Bloomsbury House, London W.C.1. on Thursday, November 25th, at 3.p.m.* National Archives (Kew), HO 294/169.
2 *History of the International Information Office Dachau.* 1.1.6.0/82089048, ITS DAWL.
3 Walter Cieslik, "Preface" to Cieslik and Ing. St. Kubalka, *Dachau* (May 1946). 5.3.3/84629700, ITS DAWL.
4 Walter Cieslik, "Preface" to Cieslik and Ing. St. Kubalka, *Dachau* (May 1946). 5.3.3/84629700, ITS DAWL.
5 International Tracing Service of IRO, *Monthly Report of the Director, No. 21, September 1949*, 7-8. ITS Bad Arolsen, NInv 1823, Box II.
6 Cieslik and Kubalka, *Dachau.* 5.3.3/84629707, ITS DAWL.

Acknowledgements

This exhibition was co-curated by Dr Christine Schmidt for The Wiener Library and Professor Dan Stone, Holocaust Research Institute, Royal Holloway, University of London, with extensive support from the International Tracing Service.

The curators are thankful for the support of the Royal Holloway Research Strategy Fund, the Leverhulme Trust, and the Library's Friends and supporters, which make its work possible. With special thanks to Elise Bath and Dr Susanne Urban for their assistance.

Made in the USA
Middletown, DE
25 August 2019